THE ART OF
GEORGE R. R. MARTIN'S
A SONG OF
ICE & FIRE

VOLUME ONE

CREDITS

REVISED EDITION EDITOR
Patricia Meredith

FIRST EDITION EDITOR
Brian Wood

FOREWORD
George R.R. Martin

CHAPTER INTRODUCTIONS
Pat Harrigan

REVISED EDITION QUOTE TEAM
Nate French

FIRST EDITION QUOTE TEAM
Tim Sturm, Jon Cazares, Geoff Daniel, Mike Dockerty, Jason Grall, Andy Kluis, Brian Wood

REVISED EDITION COPYEDITING
Kevin Tomczyk

FIRST EDITION COPYEDITING
James Torr

COVER ILLUSTRATION
Tomasz Jedruszek and Michael Komarck

REVISED EDITION INTERIOR ILLUSTRATION
Ryan Barger, Allan Bednar, Linda Bergkvist, Dean Bloomfield, Jacques Bredy, Jim Burns, Manuel Calderon, Dennis Calero, Michael Capprotti, Jhoneil Centeno, Miguel Coimbra, Daarken, Thomas Denmark, Chris Dien, Jenny Dolfen, Allen Douglas, Emrah Elmasli, Jason Engle, Mark Evans, Anders Finér, Mike Franchina, Donato Giancola, Thomas Gianni, John Gravato, Cris Griffin, Daerick Gross, Sr., Nils Hamm, Bjarne Hansen, John Howe, Christian Iken, Uwe Jarling, Tomasz Jedruszek, Scott Keating, Patrick Keith, Michel Koch, Michael Komarck, Graig Kreindler, Henning Ludvigsen, Don Maitz, Roberto Marchesi, John Matson, Patrick McEvoy, Franz Miklis, Mike S. Miller, Socar Myles, Andrew Navaro, Torstein Nordstrand, Roman V. Papsuev, Jim Pavelic, Ted Pendergraft, Martina Pilcerova, Esad Ribic, Natascha Roeoesli, John Schoenherr, Marc Simonetti, Jamie Sims, Steve Stone, Xia Taptara, J.P. Targete, Jean Tay, Sedone Thongvilay, Tim Truman, Charles Vess, Franz Vohwinkel, Shane Watson, Eric Wilkerson, Stephen Youll

GRAPHIC DESIGN
Andrew Navaro

REVISED EDITION EXECUTIVE DEVELOPER
Michael Hurley

FIRST EDITION EXECUTIVE DEVELOPER
Greg Benage

PUBLISHER
Christian T. Petersen

Contents

Foreword by George R.R. Martin   **4**

HISTORY   **6**
*Images from Aegon's conquest to the
overthrow of the Targaryen Dynasty
in the year 283*

THE NORTH   **20**
*Images of the lands above the Neck,
including Houses Stark, Umber, and Karstark*

THE WALL AND BEYOND   **42**
*Images of the sworn brothers of the Night's
Watch, the Wildlings, and other beings
beyond the Wall*

IRON ISLANDS   **62**
Images of the Greyjoys and the islands of the ironmen

KINGDOM OF MOUNTAIN AND VALE   **78**
*Images of the Vale of Arryn, including House
Arryn and the clansmen of the Mountains
of the Moon*

THE RIVERLANDS   **86**
*Images of the lands around the Neck, including
House Tully, House Frey, and the various
outlaws and battles fought there*

THE WESTERLANDS   **102**
*Images of the lands of Houses Lannister,
Clegane, and Payne*

THE STORMLANDS   **114**
*Images of the eastern shore, including Dragonstone
and Houses Baratheon and Tarth*

KING'S LANDING   **130**
*Images of the heart of Westeros and the seat
of the Iron Throne*

THE REACH   **150**
Images of the lands and people of House Tyrell

DORNE   **158**
Images of the lands and people of House Martell

THE FREE CITIES & THE EAST   **168**
*Images from beyond the lands of Westeros,
including the last surviving Targaryens*

ARTIST BIOS   **184**

FOREWORD

by George R. R. Martin

It was not entirely without trepidation that I gave Fantasy Flight Games the rights to do a board game and collectible card game based on my fantasy series, *A Song of Ice and Fire*.

That they would create good games, I had no doubt. Before I accepted the offer I'd had extensive discussions with Fantasy Flight about the approach they wanted to take to adapt my novels for gaming. I felt that I was in good hands, that Fantasy Flight would create excellent games while remaining faithful to the spirit and essence of my books. As indeed they have.

It wasn't the details of rules and game play that concerned me. It was the fact that I knew these games would both require artwork. The collectible card game, in particular, would require lots and lots and **lots** of artwork. Every card would have a picture, and there were going to be hundreds and thousands of cards. My world and characters were about to be **illustrated**, big time.

That's a prospect that would make any writer nervous.

Mind you, I love illustrated books, and always have. I started out as a comic book fan, after all, and once aspired to write "funny books" (and even draw them, an aspiration derailed by a total inability to draw). Even "real books" often featured artwork during my childhood; a frontispiece at the very least, and often more. I still can't think of *Treasure Island* or *Robin Hood* without remembering the wonderful N.C. Wyeth artwork that helped bring them to life.

I loved stories and I loved pictures, and it seemed to me that the two of them belonged together, like peanut butter and jelly, Abbott and Costello, milk and cookies. You could have cookies without milk, or Costello without Abbott, sure, but why? They worked so well together . . . and so did words and pictures.

Of course, when the words in question are **your** words, sometimes you feel a little different, as I discovered when I grew up and became a writer.

"You're going to love the cover," they always tell you. It is one of the great lies of publishing, second only to, "Your check is in the mail." You want to believe them, but you can't. The check is never in the mail, and more

often that not, you don't love the cover. Is that supposed to be your hero? It doesn't look a thing like him. Why are there two moons in the sky? Is that a unicorn peering from the trees? There are no unicorns in your novel. Why does your heroine have breasts the size of beach balls? Did the artist even **read** the book???

More often than not the answer is, "No, he didn't." A lot of covers are painted from brief paragraph-long (if that) descriptions of the scene the art director wants to feature. Maybe the cover wasn't painted for your book at all, just plucked from the Big Bin of Generic Fantasy Art the publisher keeps down in the basement. Even the Giants of Our Field are not immune to having strange or inappropriate covers put on their books. J.R.R. Tolkien himself had to wonder why there were emus on the cover of the American edition of *The Hobbit*.

All things considered, I have been luckier than most. At the start of my career, I was fortunate enough to have my work illustrated by a veritable "Who's Who" of top artists. Some of my early *Analog* cover stories were blessed with paintings by Paul Lehr, Frank Kelly Freas, Jack Gaughan, Vincent diFate, and John Schoenherr, each more gorgeous than the last. When Avon published my first book in 1976, they went outside the field to the British artist Patrick Woodroffe who produced a cover strange, surreal, and unforgettable. On my Haviland Tuf series, I was given the wonderful Janet Aulisio, the definitive Tuf artist, who captured the character just as I had imagined him. And when my historical horror novel *Fevre Dream* came out in 1982, it was graced with a stunning cover by Barron Storey, the original of which hangs on my living room wall today. A haunting and beautiful painting . . . even though Storey did feature a sternwheeler, while the steamer in the novel is actually a sidewheeler . . .

Which illustrates the problem. Any writer worth reading **lives** his stories, for months and even years. My own work has always had a strong visual component. My aim is to put my readers into the scene, so they feel as if they are experiencing the events of the story rather than just being told about them. When I write a scene, I see it vividly: the characters, the setting, the actions, everything. Of course, to keep the narrative moving, much of this has to be described in broad strokes, or else the book would bog down in a morass of details. You want to give them a sense of what a character looks like, without stopping the story dead to count his nose hairs and the number of buttons on his doublet. For the rest, you rely on the imagination of the reader. . .

. . . or the artist.

And that, of course, is a big part of what makes being illustrated a potentially nerve-wracking experience for a writer. The artist must fill in all those missing details, and the odds are good that he or she is not going to fill them in the same way you did inside your head when you were giving birth to these characters. You are trusting your children to a stranger, hoping he will treat them gently.

Or, in the case of Fantasy Flight, to a veritable army of strangers. A few of the artists they brought on board were folks I had worked with before. Most were not, and I really had no idea of what kind of work they would give me.

Would I know Ned when I saw him? Would Jaime have the same arrogant smile he has in the books? Would the King's Landing on the card match the King's Landing inside my head? All I could do was hope . . . and put my Seven Kingdoms into the hands of Eric Lang, Brian Wood, Christian Petersen, and the other good folks at Fantasy Flight.

I'm not sorry that I did. By now, FFG has released several starter decks, expansion sets, new editions– hundreds if not thousands of cards by dozens of different artists. Some of it has been ordinary, some generic, and a few pieces here and there have been downright awful or utterly inappropriate (though so far there have been no emus, I am pleased to say). The overall quality of the art has been good, however; much has been very good indeed, and some of the pieces have been spectacular. You hold the proof of that in your hands.

The Art of Ice and Fire contains the very best of the artwork done for Fantasy Flight's board game and collectible card game . . . and a good deal more. While I have been writing my *Feast for Crows*, they have been preparing a feast for the eyes.

Here, indeed, is the world of Westeros as I imagined it: the chilly honor of the Starks and the cruel splendor of the Lannisters, the squalor and danger of King's Landing, the sands of Dorne, the flowers of Highgarden, the snows of Winterfell, the icy immensity

of the Wall and the fiery promise of Daenerys and her dragons . . . it's all here, brought to vivid life with paint, pencil, or pixel by John Howe, John Schoenherr, Michael Komarck, Jim Burns, Stephen Youll, Don Maitz, Donato Giancola, John Matson, Thomas Denmark, Martina Pilcerova, Roman V. Papsuev, Franz Miklis, Steve Stone, Mike S. Miller, and a host of other gifted artists too numerous to mention.

My only complaint about *The Art of Ice and Fire* is that it is way too short. I would have liked another hundred pages . . . there was lots of terrific artwork that we had to leave out, and given more time and more space, we could have commissioned more originals as well. But who knows? The card game and the board game both continue, so in a few more years we may well have enough work for *The Art of Ice and Fire, Volume Two*. Westeros is very large, after all, and there are many places to visit, and people yet to meet...

George R.R. Martin, September, 2005

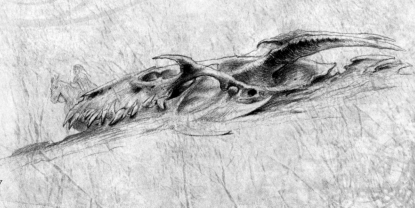

Dragon Skull • John Howe • © John Howe

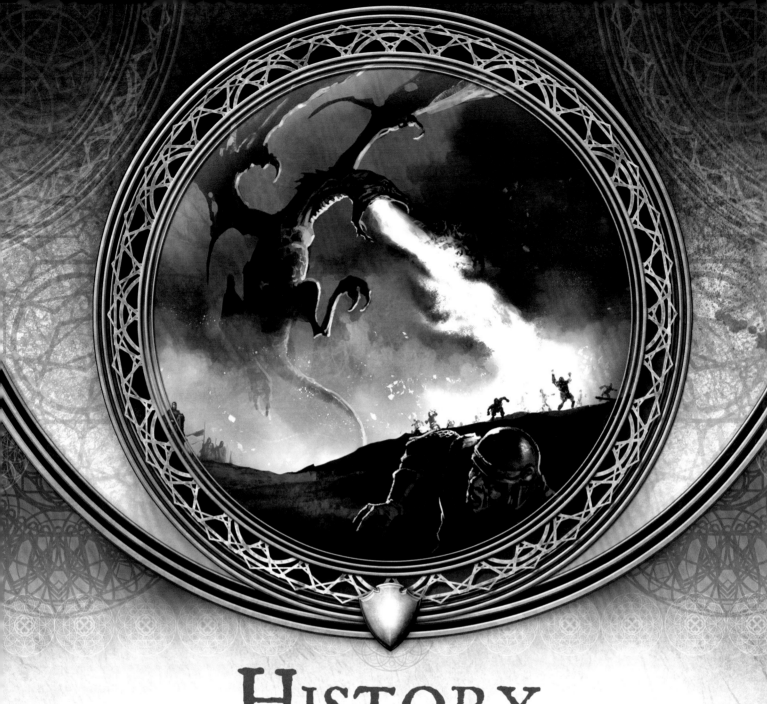

HISTORY

In the Dawn Age of Westeros there lived the Children of the Forest, about whom little is known. Then from the East came the First Men, who fought many battles with the Children before finding peace with them. Then came the Andals and the Rhoynar, and over the millennia these races fought and died and mingled and merged–except for the Children, who retreated farther into their forests and were lost from history. Eventually a land of seven kingdoms arose.

This uneasy stability lasted until the arrival of the Targaryen conqueror Aegon and his two sisters. The Targaryens traced their bloodline back beyond the island of Dragonstone to mysterious, doomed Valyria, and they brought to this new continent their dreams of conquest.

And they brought their dragons.

The Targaryen dynasty lasted hundreds of years, until the rebellion of the Usurper Robert Baratheon, and the death of Mad King Aerys by the sword of Jaime Lannister, the Kingslayer.

Daenerys I • by Roman V. Papsuev

"For centuries the Targaryens had married brother to sister, since Aegon the Conqueror had taken his sisters to bride."

Aegon, Visenya, and Rhaenys • by John Schoenherr • © John Schoenherr

"Rhaegar lost on the Trident. He lost the battle, he lost the war, he lost the kingdom, and he lost his life. His blood swirled downriver with the rubies from his breastplate, and Robert the Usurper rode over his corpse to steal the Iron Throne. Rhaegar fought valiantly, Rhaegar fought nobly, Rhaegar fought honorably. And Rhaegar *died.*"

—Ser Jorah Mormont, *A Storm of Swords*

Rhaegar Targaryen • by Anders Finér

"'What Aerys did to your brother Brandon was unspeakable. The way your lord father died, that was unspeakable. And Rhaegar… how many times do you think he raped your sister? How many hundreds of times?' His voice had grown so loud that his horse whinnied nervously beneath him. The king jerked the reins hard, quieting the animal, and pointed an angry finger at Ned. 'I will kill every Targaryen I can get my hands on, until they are as dead as their dragons, and then I will piss on their graves.'"

Mad King Aerys • by John Howe • © John Howe

Viserys Targaryen • by Mark Evans

9

Battle on the Trident • by Mike S. Miller

"Aegon's dragons were named for the gods of Old Valyria.

Visenya's dragon was Vhagar, Rhaenys had Meraxes, and Aegon rode Balerion, the Black Dread."

Vhagar • by Anders Finér

Meraxes • by Anders Finér

"It was said that Vhagar's breath was so hot that it could melt a knight's armor and cook the man inside, that Meraxes swallowed horses whole, and Balerion...his fire was as black as his scales, his wings so vast that whole towns were swallowed up in their shadow when he passed overhead."

"You could have ridden a horse down Vhagar's gullet, although you would not have ridden it out again. Meraxes was even bigger."

Consumed by Flame • by J. P. Targete

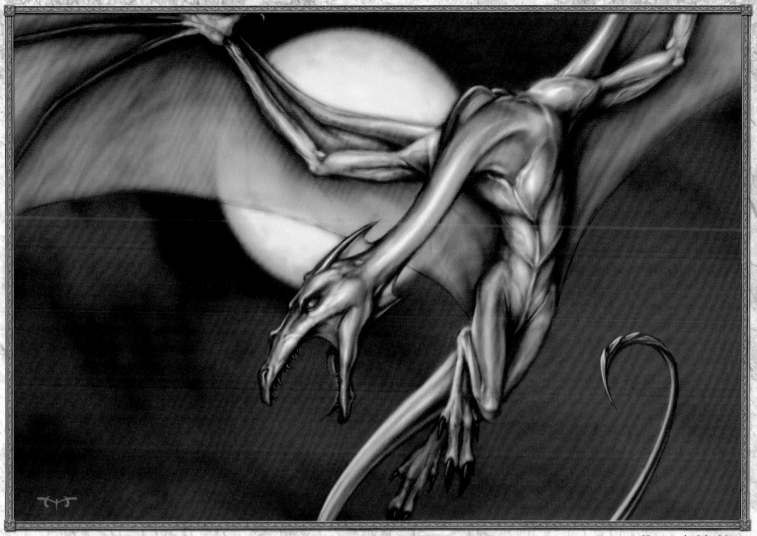

Viserion • by John Matson

"And the greatest of them, Balerion, the Black Dread, could have swallowed an aurochs whole, or even one of the hairy mammoths said to roam the cold wastes beyond the Port of Ibben."

Dragon Sight • by Tomasz Jedruszek

Aerion Brightflame • by Mike S. Miller • © Dabel Brothers Productions

Baelor Targaryen • by Mike S. Miller • © Dabel Brothers Productions

"Septons, lords, and smallfolk had turned a blind eye to the Targaryens for hundreds of years..."

"My brother sold me to Khal Drogo for the promise of a golden crown. Well, Drogo crowned him in gold, though not as he had wished, and I... My sun-and-stars made a queen of me, but if he had been a different man, it might have been much otherwise. Do you think I have forgotten how it felt to be afraid?"

–Daenerys Targaryen, *A Storm of Swords*

Seductive Promise • by Andrew Navaro

The Tower of Joy • by Torstein Nordstrand

"It was the only time Vhagar, Meraxes, and Balerion were all unleashed at once. The singers called it the Field of Fire.

Near four thousand men had burned that day..."

Bathed in Flame • by Tomasz Jedruszek

"'I would name them all for those the gods have taken. The green one shall be Rhaegal, for my valiant brother who died on the green banks of the Trident. The cream-and-gold I call Viserion. Viserys was cruel and weak and frightened, yet he was my brother still. His dragon will do what he could not.'

'And the black beast?' asked Ser Jorah Mormont.

'The black,' she said, 'is Drogon.'"

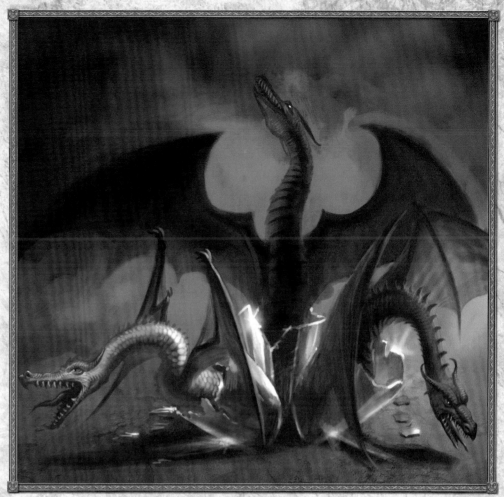

Hatchlings • by Thomas Denmark

"Dany listened to the talk in the streets, and she heard these things, but she knew better than to question her brother when he wove his web of dream. His anger was a terrible thing when roused. Viserys called it 'waking the dragon.'"

Viserys Targaryen • by John Matson

Knights • by Mike S. Miller

Knights • by Anders Finér

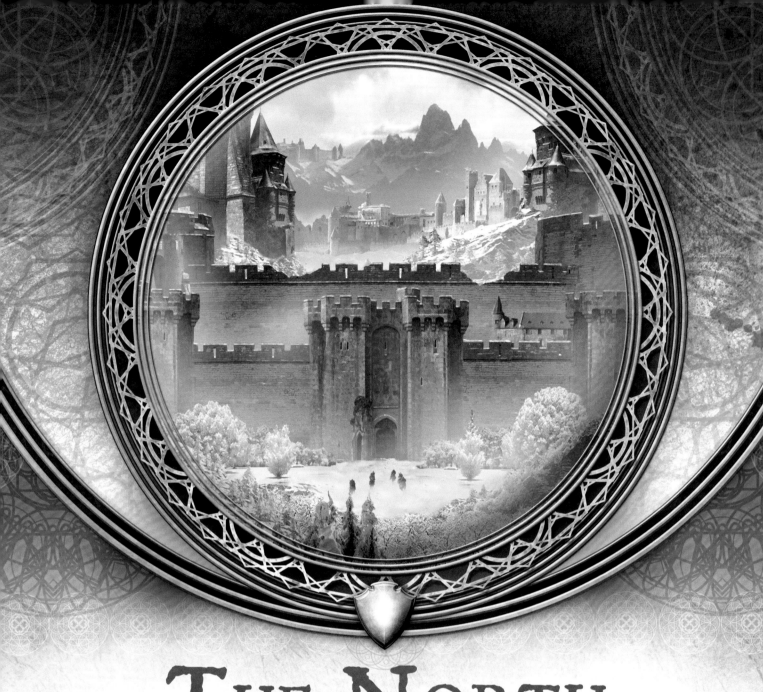

THE NORTH

The First Men settled in the North of the continent, and its bleak, forbidding landscape suited the hard, unforgiving men who built their lives there.

The Starks of Winterfell ruled this land, proud, aloof, and austere, until Aegon and his dragons arrived in Westeros, and then the last King in the North reluctantly bent the knee to the Targaryen despot, and the North became one of the Seven Kingdoms.

But in this cold land, memories are long, and a new King in the North may someday arise and call to himself his bannermen: the Boltons, the Umbers, the Karstarks, and the Mormonts, and reclaim the North for the descendents of the First Men.

Winterfell Throne • by Marc Simonetti

"I despaired of ever making a lady of [Arya]. She collected scabs as other girls collected dolls and would say anything that came into her head."

–Catelyn Stark, *A Clash of Kings*

"[Rickon] had refused to let anyone cut [his hair] since their mother had gone. The last girl to try had been bitten for her efforts."

Arya Stark • by Mark Evans

"Once Bran had known every stone of those buildings, inside and out; he had climbed them all, scampering up walls as easily as other boys ran down stairs. Their rooftops had been his secret places, and the crows atop the broken tower his special friends.

And then he had fallen."

"You have five trueborn children," Jon said. "Three sons, two daughters. The direwolf is the sigil of your House. Your children were meant to have these pups, my lord."

Rickon Stark • by Mark Evans

Bran Stark • by Mark Evans

Jon Snow • by Natascha Roeoesli

Direwolf Pups • by Jenny Dolfen • © Jenny Dolfen

"Sansa could sew and dance and sing. She wrote poetry. She knew how to dress. She played the high harp *and* the bells. Worse, she was beautiful. Sansa had gotten her mother's fine high cheekbones and the thick auburn hair of the Tullys."

Hodor and Bran • by Jamie Sims • © Testor Corporation

Sansa Stark • by Mark Evans

"Yet our way is the older way. The blood of the First Men still flows in the veins of the Starks, and we hold to the belief that the man who passes the sentence should swing the sword."

–Eddard Stark, *A Game of Thrones*

Eddard Stark • by Allan Bednar

"'They say it grows so cold up here in winter that a man's laugh freezes in his throat and chokes him to death,' Ned said evenly. 'Perhaps that is why the Starks have so little humor.'"

Eddard Stark • by John Matson

"As hard as birth can be, Brienne, what comes after is even harder. At times I feel as if I am being torn apart. Would that there were five of me, one for each child, so I might keep them all safe."

–Catelyn Stark, *A Clash of Kings*

Catelyn Stark • by Mark Evans

Arya • by Jamie Sims • © Testor Corporation

"All his garb was green, even to the leather of his boots, and when he came close, Bran saw his eyes were the color of moss, though his teeth looked as white as anyone else's. Both Reeds were slight of build, slender as swords and scarcely taller than Bran himself."

Jojen Reed • by Roman V. Papsuev

"Though near Robb's age, she was slim as a boy, with long brown hair knotted behind her head and only the barest suggestion of breasts."

Meera Reed • by Roman V. Papsuev

Three-Eyed Crow • by John Howe • © John Howe

"That won't do any good, the crow said. *I told you, the answer is flying, not crying. How hard can it be? I'm doing it.* The crow took to the air and flapped around Bran's hand.

'You have wings,' Bran pointed out.

Maybe you do, too."

"Little Rickon called his Shaggydog, which Bran thought was a pretty stupid name for a direwolf."

Shaggydog • by John Matson

"Tears were streaming down the maester's face, yet he shook his head doggedly. 'The children...live only in dreams. Now. Dead and gone. Enough, that's enough...'

'Old Nan says the children knew the songs of the trees, that they could fly like birds and swim like fish and talk to the animals,' Bran said. 'She says that they made music so beautiful that it made you cry like a little baby just to hear it.'"

The Things I Do For Love • by Martina Pilcerova

Maester Luwin • by Mark Evans

"Luwin was always tucking things into those sleeves and producing other things from them: books, messages, strange artifacts, toys for the children. With all he kept hidden in his sleeves, Catelyn was surprised Maester Luwin could lift his arms at all."

Northern Champion • by John Gravato

Greatjon Umber • by John Matson

"Cursing, the Greatjon flung a flagon of ale into the fire and bellowed that Robb was so green he must piss grass. When Hallis Mollen moved to restrain him, he knocked him to the floor, kicked over a table, and unsheathed the biggest, ugliest greatsword that Bran had ever seen."

Lookout • by Jacques Bredy

"Jory's sword was already out. 'Robb, get away from it!' he called as his horse reared under him. Robb grinned and looked up from the bundle in his arms. 'She can't hurt you,' he said. 'She's dead, Jory.'"

Jory Cassell • by John Matson

Rodrik Cassell • by Roman V. Papsuev

"They were huffing and puffing and hitting at each other with padded wooden swords under the watchful eye of old Ser Rodrik Cassel, the master-at-arms, a great stout keg of a man with magnificent white cheek whiskers."

"In the name of Robert of the House Baratheon, the First of his Name, King of the Andals and the Rhoynar and the First Men, Lord of the Seven Kingdoms and Protector of the Realm, by the word of Eddard of the House Stark, Lord of Winterfell and Warden of the North, I do sentence you to die."

—Eddard Stark, *A Game of Thrones*

Winterfell Audience Chamber • by Torstein Nordstrand

John and Ghost • by Cris Griffin

A Game of Thrones • by Stephen Youll • © Stephen Youll

"'Your Grace,' Ned said respectfully. He swept the lantern in a wide semicircle. Shadows moved and lurched. Flickering light touched the stones underfoot and brushed against a long procession of granite pillars that marched ahead, two by two, into the dark. Between the pillars, the dead sat on their stone thrones against the walls, backs against the sepulchers that contained their mortal remains."

Karhold • by Franz Miklis

As Hard as the Winter • by J. P. Targete

Moat Calin • by Martina Pilcerova

38

Winterfell Castle • by Torstein Nordstrand

"The vanguard spread out behind them, a slow-moving forest of lances and banners and spears."

Robb's Sworn Swords • by Tomasz Jedruszek

"In the south, the way they talk about my seven kingdoms, a man forgets that your part is as big as the other six combined."

–Robert Baratheon, *A Game of Thrones*

Blood of the First Men • by Thomas Denmark

The Dreadfort • by Franz Miklis

Winterfell • by Steve Stone • © Steve Stone

THE WALL AND BEYOND

The Wall has stood for thousands of years. This far north, its ice will never melt; instead it grows ever larger, as generations of the Night's Watch extend and broaden it.

The Black Brothers of the Night's Watch have forsworn marriage and family; their lives are given over to one purpose alone: to defend the Seven Kingdoms from the threat beyond the Wall. They are the swords in the darkness, the shields that guard the realms of men.

There are those who live beyond the Wall, called Wildlings. They have their own cultures, rituals, rulers, and history, and are fiercely proud of their freedom. Many, even the Black Brothers, believe that they are the threat the Wall was built to defend against. They are wrong.

There are Others.

Scouting the Pass • by Esad Ribic • © Esad Ribic

Benjen Stark • by Mark Evans

"Benjen Stark stood up. 'More's the pity.'
He put a hand on Jon's shoulder. 'Come
back to me after you've fathered a few
bastards of your own, and we'll see how
you feel.'"

Fields of Ice • by Martina Pilcerova

"I knew Mance Rayder, Jon. He is an oathbreaker, yes... but he has eyes to see, and no man has ever dared to name him faintheart."

–Old Bear Mormont, *A Clash of Kings*

Mance Rayder • by Anders Finér

Mance Rayder • by Allen Douglas

"The wildlings did not make captives of the men they called the crows. They killed them, except for... 'They only spare oathbreakers. Those who join them, like Mance Rayder.'"

–Jon Snow, *A Clash of Kings*

Beyond the Wall • by Charles Vess • © Charles Vess

Sworn Brother • by Thomas Denmark

"Far off to the north, a wolf began to howl. Another voice picked up the call, then another. Ghost cocked his head and listened. 'If he doesn't come back,' Jon Snow promised, 'Ghost and I will go find him.' He put his hand on the direwolf's head."

Jon Snow • by Roman V. Papsuev

"We could use a man like you on the Wall..."

–Benjen Stark, *A Game of Thrones*

Marched to the Wall • by Tim Truman

"The cold winds are rising, and men go out from their fires and never come back...or if they do, they're not men no more, but only wights, with blue eyes and cold, black hands."

–Osha, *A Game of Thrones*

Wight • by Anders Finér

"And there is the Wall. You need to see it, Your Grace, to walk along its battlements and talk to those who man it. The Night's Watch is a shadow of what it once was."

–Eddard Stark, *A Game of Thrones*

Castle Black • by Martina Pilcerova

Fallen Brother • by Thomas Denmark

The Wall is Yours • by Jenny Dolfen • © Jenny Dolfen

"Jon could see the Wall looming high and dark to the south, a great shadow blocking out the stars. The rough hilly ground made him think they must be somewhere between the Shadow Tower and Castle Black..."

Shadow Tower • by Franz Miklis

Old Bear Mormont • by Jamie Sims • © Testor Corporation

"'It's no freak,' Jon said calmly. 'That's a direwolf. They grow larger than the other kind.'"

Mark of the Wolf • by Anders Finér

"Sometimes he could sense them, though, as if they were still with him, only hidden from his sight by a boulder or a stand of trees. He could not smell them, nor hear their howls by night, yet he felt their presence at his back ..."

At Night They Howl • by Jhoneil Centeno

"You want us to travel a longer road on foot, without even knowing where it ends. Beyond the Wall, you say. I haven't been there, no more than you, but I know that Beyond the Wall's a big place, Jojen."

—Meera Reed, *A Storm of Swords*

Wolfswood Hunters • by Tomasz Jedruszek

First Ranging • by J. P. Targete

"'There are abandoned castles along the Wall, I've heard,' Jojen answered. 'Fortresses built by the Night's Watch but now left empty. One of them may give us our way through.'"

Brandon's Gift • by Martina Pilcerova

"Then all of them were drawing, and it was near three hundred upraised swords and as many voices crying, 'The horn that wakes the sleepers! The shield that guards the realms of men!' Chett had no choice but to join his voice to the others. The air was misty with their breath, and firelight glinted off the steel."

Defenders of the North • by Ryan Barger

"The Halfhand had suspected that the wildlings had gone up into the bleak and barren Frostfangs in search of some weapon, some power, some fell sorcery with which to break the Wall…"

Frostfangs • by Franz Miklis

"The fear that filled Sam then was worse than any fear he had ever felt before, and Samwell Tarly knew every kind of fear."

Samwell Tarly • by Roman V. Papsuev

"When the dead walk, walls and stakes and swords mean nothing. You cannot fight the dead, Jon Snow. No man knows that half so well as me."

–Mance Rayder, *A Storm of Swords*

Winter is Coming • by Thomas Denmark

"At evenfall, as the sun sets and we face the gathering night, you shall take your vows. From that moment, you will be a Sworn Brother of the Night's Watch. Your crimes will be washed away, your debts forgiven. So too you must wash away your former loyalties, put aside your grudges, forget old wrongs and loves alike. Here you begin anew."

–Old Bear Mormont, *A Game of Thrones*

Wolfswood • by Franz Miklis

Take the Black • by Mark Evans

Wildling Armies • by Anders Finér

Tormund Giantsbane • by Anders Finér

"Every night when they made camp, Ygritte threw her sleeping skins down beside his own, no matter if he was near the fire or well away from it. Once he woke to find her nestled against him, her arm across his chest."

Ygritte • by Roman V. Papsuev

"There was no leaving the Night's Watch, once you said your words. Anywhere in the Seven Kingdoms, they'd take you and kill you."

Ruthless Defender • by Roman V. Papsuev

"His father's gods, he said, but they are wildling gods, as well."

Wildling Elder • by Miguel Coimbra

"'A crow come over,' said Rattleshirt, who preferred to be called the Lord of Bones, for the clattering armor he wore. 'He was afraid I'd take his bones as well as Halfhand's.' He shook his sack of trophies at the other wildlings."

Lord of Bones • by Anders Finér

"We met with Alfyn Crowkiller. Mance had sent him to scout along the Wall, and we chanced on him returning... Alfyn will trouble the realm no longer, but some of his company escaped us. We hunted down as many as we could, but it may be that a few will win back to the mountains."

–Qhorin Halfhand, *A Clash of Kings*

Alfyn Crowkiller • by Henning Ludvigsen

Disgraced Lordling • by Jean Tay

Grenn • by Jason Engle

"Grenn was sixteen and a head taller than Jon. All four of them were bigger than he was, but they did not scare him. He'd beaten every one of them in the yard."

60

Mammoth Riders • by Jim Burns • © Jim Burns

IRON ISLANDS

The Greyjoys of Pyke never truly accepted the authority of the Iron Throne. The ruling family of the Ironborn, and all their subjects, are reavers and warriors at heart. As they would have it, each captain is king of his own ship and the only possessions worth having are those paid for with the iron price: with sword and blood.

Before Aegon's Conquest, the Ironborn controlled much of the western shores of the continent, but under Targaryen rule they were forced back to sea, and they now scratch out a meager living from the salt-crusted rocks of Pyke, Harlaw, Saltcliffe, and the other desolate islands.

Now, as the lords of Westeros struggle for control of the Iron Throne, the Ironborn strike again, hoping to seize control of whatever they can, and burn what they cannot.

The Seastone Chair • by Marc Simonetti

"Theon shifted his seat. 'My uncle Euron has not been seen in the islands for close on two years. He may be dead. If so, it might be for the best. Lord Balon's eldest brother had never given up the Old Way, even for a day. His *Silence*, with its black sails and dark red hull, was infamous in every port from Ibben to Asshai, it was said.'"

Euron Crow's Eye • by Roman V. Papsuev

Theon Greyjoy • by Nils Hamm

Euron Crow's Eye • by Patrick McEvoy

"Crow's Eye, you call me. Well, who has a keener eye than the crow? After every battle the crows come in their hundreds and their thousands to feast upon the fallen. A crow can espy death from afar. And I say that all of Westeros is dying."

–Euron Crow's Eye, *A Feast for Crows*

Longship Kraken • by Daerick Gross, Sr.

"And from this day on, I want a careful watch kept over Theon Greyjoy. If there is war, we shall have sore need of his father's fleet."

–Eddard Stark, *A Game of Thrones*

Ironman's Bay • by Franz Miklis

65

"I am the Greyjoy, Lord Reaper of Pyke, King of Salt and Rock, Son of the Sea Wind, and no man gives me a crown."

–Balon Greyjoy, *A Clash of Kings*

Every Captain a King • by Anders Finér

"The Iron Islands lived in the past; the present was too hard and bitter to be borne."

Ironborn Captain • by Patrick McEvoy

Balon Greyjoy • by Anders Finér

Balon Greyjoy • by Jim Pavelic

"Aeron Greyjoy had been the most amiable of his uncles, feckless and quick to laugh, fond of songs, ale, and women."

Greyjoy Councilor • by Emrah Elmasli

"'Bless him with salt, bless him with stone, bless him with steel. Nephew, do you still know the words?'

'What is dead may never die,' Theon said, remembering.

'What is dead may never die,' his uncle echoed, 'but rises again, harder and stronger.'"

Aeron Damphair • by Patrick McEvoy

Aeron Damphair • by Anders Finér

Theon Greyjoy • by Mark Evans

Summer Sea Brigands • by Michael Capprotti

MARTINA 2002

The Sea Tower • by Martina Pilcerova

"Theon might have been impressed if he had not known that these were the very chambers that had given the Bloody Keep its name. A thousand years before, the sons of the River King had been slaughtered here, hacked to bits in their beds, so that pieces of their bodies might be sent back to their father on the mainland."

Kings of Salt and Rock • by Anders Finér

The Bloody Keep • by Martina Pilcerova

"Balon Greyjoy's wife is elderly and failing, but such a match would commit us to an alliance with the Iron Islands, and I am still uncertain whether that would be our wisest course."

–Tywin Lannister, *A Storm of Swords*

Alannys Greyjoy • by Henning Ludvigsen

The Lonely Light • by Martina Pilcerova

The Knight Greyjoy • by Roman V. Papsuev

"To be a knight, you must stand your vigil in a sept, and be anointed with the seven oils to consecrate your vows. In the north, only a few of the great houses worship the Seven. The rest honor the old gods, and name no knights...but those lords and their sons and sworn swords are no less fierce or loyal or honorable. A man's worth is not marked by a ser before his name."

–Maester Luwin, *A Game of Thrones*

Pyke • by John Howe • © John Howe

The Burden of Conquest • by Manuel Calderon

"Under a snowy white mane of hair, Dagmer Cleftjaw had the most gut-churning scar Theon had ever seen, the legacy of the longaxe that had near killed him as a boy. The blow had splintered his jaw, shattered his front teeth, and left him four lips where other men had but two. A shaggy beard covered his cheeks and neck, but the hair would not grow over the scar, so a shiny seam of puckered, twisted flesh divided his face like a crevasse through a snowfield."

Cleftjaw Reavers • by Tomasz Jedruszek

"We are the ironborn, and once we were conquerors. Our writ ran everywhere the sound of waves was heard. My brother would have you be content with the cold and dismal north, my niece with even less...but I shall give you Lannisport. Highgarden. The Arbor. Oldtown. The Riverlands, and the Reach, the kingswood and the rainwood, Dorne and the marches, the Mountains of the Moon and the Vale of Arryn, Tarth and the Stepstones. I say we take it all! I say, we take Westeros."

—Euron Crow's Eye, *A Feast for Crows*

King Euron's Horde • by Tomasz Jedruszek

Iron Islands • by Franz Miklis

Iron Coast • by Franz Miklis

Ironborn • by Anders Finér

"'Oh, that part was true enough.' Asha leapt to her feet. 'Rolfe, here,' she shouted down at one of the finger dancers, holding up a hand. He saw her, spun, and suddenly an axe came flying from his hand, the blade gleaming as it tumbled end over end through the torchlight. Theon had time for a choked gasp before Asha snatched the axe from the air and slammed it down into the table, splitting his trencher in two and splattering his mantle with drippings. 'There's my lord husband.' His sister reached down inside her gown and drew a dirk from between her breasts. 'And here's my sweet suckling babe.'"

Iron Mines • by Franz Miklis

KINGDOM OF MOUNTAIN AND VALE

The seven white towers of the Eyrie command the Vale of Arryn, and at the top of this impossibly tall–and, they say, impregnable–fortress rules the family of Arryn. Any traveler who seeks audience with the lords or ladies of Arryn must pass through the Gates of the Moon, and then climb the mountain, through the gates of Stone, the gates of Snow, and the gates of Sky, and up further still to the Eyrie.

Those who displease Lady Lysa Arryn may find the way down considerably shorter.

This rough country is also home to lawless bands of clansmen–the Moon Brothers, the Stone Crows, the Black Ears, the Burned Men–and even the lords of the Vale must ride in strength when they leave the safety of the Eyrie, lest they be kidnapped or murdered.

The Eyrie • by John Howe • © John Howe

Mountains of the Moon • by Franz Miklis

"On the far side of the stoneworks, the mountains opened up suddenly upon a vista of green fields, blue sky, and snow-capped mountains that took her breath away. The Vale of Arryn bathed in the morning light. It stretched before them to the misty east, a tranquil land of rich black soil, wide, slow-moving rivers, and hundreds of small lakes that shone like mirrors in the sun, protected on all sides by its sheltering peaks."

The Eyrie • by Martina Pilcerova

Sky Cell • by Anders Finér

Robert Arryn • by Anders Finér

"'M'lord Varys complimented Chella on her ears and said she must have killed many men to have such a fine necklace,' Shae explained. It grated on him to hear her call Varys m'lord in that tone; that was what she called him in their pillow play. 'And Chella told him only cowards kill the vanquished.'"

Chella • by Sedone Thongvilay

Chella, Daughter of Cheyk • by Cris Griffin

Chella, Daughter of Cheyk • by Thomas Gianni

"'Why should we trust your word?' Chella was a small, hard woman, flat as a boy, and no fool. 'Lowland lords have lied to the clans before.'"

"I will cut off your manhood and feed it to the goats."

–Shagga, Son of Dolf, *A Game of Thrones*

Shagga, Son of Dolf • by Roman V. Papsuev

Bronn • by Jason Engle

Lysa Arryn • by Roman V. Papsuev

"'My lords, with your leave, I propose to travel to the Vale and there woo and win Lady Lysa Arryn. Once I am her consort, I shall deliver you the Vale of Arryn without a drop of blood being spilled.'

Lord Rowan looked doubtful. 'Would Lady Lysa have you?'

'She's had me a few times before, Lord Mathis, and voiced no complaints.'

'Bedding,' said Cersei, 'is not wedding. Even a cow like Lysa Arryn might be able to grasp the difference.'"

"Ser Vardis turned his side to his foe, trying to use his shield to block instead, but Bronn slid around him, quick as a cat. The sellsword seemed to be getting stronger. His cuts were leaving their marks now. Deep shiny gashes gleamed all over the knight's armor, on his right thigh, his beaked visor, crossing on his breastplate, a long one along the front of his gorget. The moon-and-falcon rondel over Ser Vardis's right arm was sheared clean in half, hanging by its strap."

Bronn • by Natascha Roeoesli

THE RIVERLANDS

Before Aegon's Conquest, the riverlands belonged to Harren the Black, King of the Iron Islands, but Harren was burned alive by dragonfire at Harrenhal during Aegon's campaign. Now House Tully controls these lands, from its ancestral home of Riverrun.

On the Trident's Ruby Ford, Robert Baratheon slew Prince Rhaegar Targaryen, in the final great battle to end Targaryen rule in Westeros. The Tullys stood behind Robert's Rebellion, and now their family is bound by marriage to the Starks of the North and Arryns of the Vale.

A less secure ally for the new regime is the aged Walder Frey of the Twins and his enormous family. The Freys are numerous and wealthy, and Walder Frey is arrogant and proud, and anyone–or any army–that wishes to cross the Bridge of the Twins must pay the price.

Passage at the Twins • by Sedone Thongvilay

Battle of the Camps • by J. P. Targete

"Catelyn Stark watched the light spread, her hands resting on the delicate carved stone of the balustrade outside her window. Below her the world turned from black to indigio to green as dawn crept across fields and forests."

Catelyn • by Allan Bednar

Catelyn and Jaime • by Mike S. Miller • © Mike S. Miller

"If the Lannisters should march, Winterfell is remote and the Vale walled up behind its mountains, but Riverrun lies right in their path."

—Ser Brynden Tully, *A Game of Thrones*

Riverrun • by Franz Miklis

Dark Wings, Dark Words • by Martina Pilcerova

"'Dark wings, dark words,' Ned murmured. It was a proverb Old Nan had taught him as a boy."

"Forty years it had taken, rising like a great shadow on the shore of the lake while Harren's armies plundered his neighbors for stone, lumber, gold, and workers. Thousands of captives died in his quarries, chained to his sledges, or laboring on his five colossal towers. Men froze by winter and sweltered in summer. Weirwoods that had stood three thousand years were cut down for beams and rafters. Harren had beggared the riverlands and the Iron Islands alike to ornament his dream."

Ghost of Harrenhal • by Linda Bergkvist

"The forks of the Trident were the easiest way to move goods or men across the riverlands. In times of peace, they would have encountered fisherfolk in their skiffs, grain barges being poled downstream, merchants selling needles and bolts of cloth from floating shops, perhaps even a gaily painted mummer's boat with quilted sails of half a hundred colors, making its way upriver from village to village and castle to castle.

But the war had taken its toll…"

Blackfish • by Cris Griffin

Sworn to the Wolf King • by Linda Bergkvist

Roslin Frey • by Roman V. Papsuev

"Both of them were called Walder Frey. Big Walder said there were bunches of Walders at the Twins, all named after the boys' grandfather, Lord Walder Frey. 'We have our own names at Winterfell,' Rickon told them haughtily when he heard that."

Riverrun • by Tomasz Jedruszek

Black Walder • by Roman V. Papsuev

The Blackfish • by Roman V. Papsuev

"The Blackfish was a tall, lean man, grey of hair and precise in his movements, his clean-shaven face lined and windburnt."

"A man sees. A man knows."

—Jaqen Hagar, *A Clash of Kings*

Jaqen Hagar • by Roman V. Papsuev

Funeral • by Charles Vess • © Charles Vess

"Biter hissed at her again, displaying a mouthful of yellowed teeth filed into points. 'A man must have some name, is that not so? Biter cannot speak and Biter cannot write, yet his teeth are very sharp, so a man calls him Biter and he smiles. Are you charmed?'"

Biter • by Roman V. Papsuev • © Roman V. Papsuev

"Rorge, the noseless one, flung his drinking cup at her with a curse. His manacles made him clumsy, yet even so he would have sent the heavy pewter tankard crashing into her head if Arya hadn't leapt aside. 'You get us some beer, pimple. Now!'"

Rorge • by Roman V. Papsuev

Walder Frey • by John Matson

"'He is not reasonable,' said Catelyn. 'He is proud, and prickly to a fault. You know that. He wanted to be grandfather to a king. You will not appease him with the offer of two hoary old brigands and the second son of the fattest man in the Seven Kingdoms. Not only have you broken your oath, but you've slighted the honor of the Twins by choosing a bride from a lesser house.'"

"A man the others called the Tickler asked the questions. His face was so ordinary and his garb so plain that Arya might have thought him one of the villagers before she had seen him at his work. 'Tickler makes them howl so hard they piss themselves,' old stoop-shoulder Chiswyck told them."

The Tickler • by Franz Vohwinkel

"This great lout with the brown teeth is Lem, short for Lemoncloak. It's yellow, you see, and Lem's a sour sort."

–Tom Sevenstrings, *A Storm of Swords*

Lem Lemoncloak • by Roman V. Papsuev

"*How many monsters does Lord Tywin have?*"

–Arya Stark, *A Clash of Kings*

Sellsword • by Thomas Denmark

100

Mercy • by Mike S. Miller • © Mike S. Miller

THE WESTERLANDS

From monumental Casterly Rock hails House Lannister, which traces its lineage back to Lann the Clever himself. These Westerlands are rich with gold, and so the Lannisters have become the wealthiest of all the Great Houses.

Gold is mined in Castamere, and from beneath the Crag and the Pendric Hills, and from beneath the enormous keep named the Golden Tooth. The goldsmiths of Lannisport refine and mold it, creating the most exquisite pieces in the Seven Kingdoms.

Perhaps even more notably, the Westerlands have produced some of the most feared warriors in the realm: Ser Ilyn Payne, the court's tongueless executioner; the brothers Sandor and Ser Gregor Clegane, who are called The Hound and The Mountain That Rides; and perhaps the greatest swordsman of all, the Kingslayer, Ser Jaime Lannister.

Defenders of the King • by Tomasz Jedruszek

Tywin Lannister • by Michael Komarck

"Do you think Lord Tywin will sit idly while his daughter's head is measured for a spike? Casterly Rock will rise, and not alone."

–Littlefinger, *A Game of Thrones*

Tywin Lannister • by John Matson

Cersei Lannister • by Michael Komarck

"Prince Tommen, who was plump to begin with, seemed positively round."

Tommen Baratheon • by John Matson

Joffrey Baratheon • by John Matson

"Joffrey gave a petulant shrug. 'Your brother defeated my uncle Jaime. My mother says it was treachery and deceit. She wept when she heard. Women are all weak, even her, though she pretends she isn't. She says we need to stay in King's Landing in case my other uncles attack, but I don't care. After my name day feast, I'm going to raise a host and kill your brother myself. That's what I'll give you, Lady Sansa. Your brother's head.'"

"'I have made more mistakes than you can possibly imagine,' Ned said, 'but that was not one of them.'

'Oh, but it was, my lord,' Cersei insisted. 'When you play the game of thrones, you win or you die. There is no middle ground.'"

Hear Me Roar • by Natascha Roeoesli

105

Ser Jaime Lannister • by Michael Komarck

"Pycelle's eyes were so heavily lidded he looked half-asleep. 'My pardons, Lord Eddard. You did not come to hear foolish meanderings of a summer forgotten before your father was born. Forgive an old man his wanderings, if you would. Minds are like swords, I do fear. The old ones go to rust.'"

Grand Maester Pycelle • by John Gravato

Pycelle • by Roman V. Papsuev

"'Princess Arianne?' The girl threw her arms around her. 'Why do they call me queen? Did something bad happen to Tommen?'

'He fell in with evil men, Your Grace,' Arianne said, 'and I fear they have conspired to steal your throne.'"

Myrcella Baratheon • by Martina Pilcerova

"He was Jaime Lannister; a knight of the Kingsguard, he was the Kingslayer. No man ever called him craven. Other things they called him, yes; oathbreaker, liar, murderer. They said he was cruel, treacherous, reckless. But never craven."

"All that the gods had given to Cersei and Jaime, they had denied Tyrion. He was a dwarf, half his brother's height, struggling to keep pace on stunted legs. His head was too large for his body, with a brute's squashed-in face beneath a swollen shelf of brow. One green eye and one black one peered out from under a lank fall of hair so blonde it seemed white."

Ser Jaime Lannister • by Jason Engle

Tyrion Lannister • by Michael Komarck

Ser Gregor Clegane • by Mark Evans

"'Ser Ilyn has not been feeling talkative these past fourteen years,' Lord Renly commented with a sly smile.

Joffrey gave his uncle a look of pure loathing, then took Sansa's hands in his own. 'Aerys Targaryen had his tongue ripped out with hot pincers.'"

Ser Ilyn Payne • by Michael Capprotti

"'He speaks most eloquently with his sword, however,' the queen said, 'and his devotion to our realm is unquestioned.'"

Ser Ilyn Payne • by Mark Evans

"That task was to have been his uncle's, but solid, steady, tireless Ser Kevan Lannister had not been himself since the raven had come from Riverrun with word of his son's murder."

Ser Kevan Lannister • by Roman V. Papsuev

Ser Gregor Clegane • by Michael Komarck

Sandor Clegane • by Jim Pavelic

THE STORMLANDS

This rough, barren land is home to no major cities, but it is not uninhabited, nor undefended. There is a longstanding enmity between the people of the stormlands and the Dornishmen to the south, and the men of these lands have long known how to make war.

The ancestral home of House Baratheon is Storm's End, a massive stone tower built, it is said, to weather the wrath of the storm gods themselves.

It was at Storm's End that Robert Baratheon defeated three lords in a single day during his rebellion; and during the siege of Storm's End, Davos Seaworth braved the waters of Shipbreaker Bay to smuggle onions and other provisions to the defenders, earning knighthood and the dubious title "The Onion Knight."

Melisandre by Asshai • by Donato Giancola • © 2005 Donato Giancola

"Ser Davos, truth can be a bitter draught, even for a man like Lord Stannis. He thinks only of returning to King's Landing in the fullness of his power, to tear down his enemies and claim what is rightfully his."

–Maester Cressen, *A Clash of Kings*

Stannis's Cavalry • by Tomasz Jedruszek

"Stannis is pure iron, black and hard and strong, yes, but brittle, the way iron gets. He'll break before he bends."

–Donal Noye, *A Clash of Kings*

Seditious Plans • by Jason Engle

Stannis Baratheon • by John Matson

"Stannis Baratheon, Lord of Dragonstone, and by the grace of the gods rightful heir to the Iron Throne of the Seven Kingdoms of Westeros, was broad of shoulder and sinewy of limb, with a tightness to his face and flesh that spoke of leather cured in the sun until it was as tough as steel. Hard was the word men used when they spoke of Stannis, and hard he was. Though he was not yet five-and-thirty, only a fringe of thin black hair remained on his head, circling behind his ears like the shadow of a crown."

Stannis Baratheon • by Mark Evans

"Stannis ground his teeth, and said, 'You called and I came, my lords. Now you must live with me, or die with me. Best get used to that.'"

Stannis Baratheon • by Allen Douglas

117

The Battle of Ruby Ford • by Tomasz Jedruszek

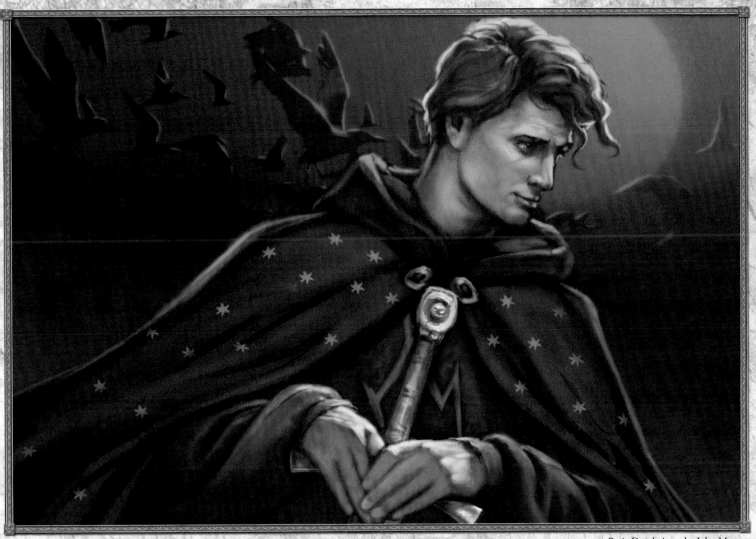

Beric Dondarion • by John Matson

"'In my dreams, I kill him every night,' Robert admitted. 'A thousand deaths will still be less than he deserves.'"

Robert Baratheon • by Chris Dien

"'A man your age must look where he steps,' Melisandre said courteously. 'The night is dark and full of terrors.'"

Melisandre • by Henning Ludvigsen

Dark Pact • by Jason Engle

Priestess • by Patrick McEvoy

"Some lights cast more than one shadow. Stand before the nightfire and you'll see for yourself. The flames shift and dance, never still. The shadows grow tall and short, and every man casts a dozen. Some are fainter than others, that's all. Well, men cast their shadows across the future as well. One shadow or many. Melisandre sees them all."

–Stannis Baratheon, *A Clash of Kings*

"The woman was the heart of it. Not the Lady Selyse, the other one. The red woman, the servants had named her, afraid to speak her name. 'I will speak her name,' Cressen told his stone hellhound. 'Melisandre. Her.' Melisandre of Asshai, sorceress, shadowbinder, and priestess to R'hllor, the Lord of Light, the Heart of Fire, the God of Flame and Shadow. Melisandre, whose madness must not be allowed to spread beyond Dragonstone."

Melisandre's Gift • by Chris Dien

Melisandre • by Chris Dien

"As ever, she wore red head to heel, a long loose gown of flowing silk as bright as fire, with jagged sleeves and deep slashes in the bodice that showed glimpses of a darker bloodred fabric beneath. Around her throat was a red gold choker tighter than any maester's chain, ornamented with a single great ruby."

Melisandre • by Mark Evans

121

Brienne, Maiden of Tarth • by John Matson

"Don't presume to judge what you do not understand, wench."

"My name is - "

" - Brienne, yes. Has anyone ever told you that you're as tedious as you are ugly?"

"You will not provoke me to anger, Kingslayer."

"Oh, I might, if I cared enough to try."

"Robert Baratheon had always been a man of huge appetites, a man who knew how to take his pleasures. That was not a charge anyone could lay at the door of Eddard Stark. Yet Ned could not help but notice that those pleasures were taking a toll on the king."

Robert Baratheon • by Henning Ludvigsen

122

Brienne and Loras Melee • by Anders Finér

Brienne, Maiden of Tarth • by Chris Dien

"Five more castles he built, each larger and stronger than the last, only to see them smashed asunder when the gale winds came howling up Shipbreaker Bay, driving great walls of water before them. His lords pleaded with him to build inland; his priests told him he must placate the gods by giving Elenei back to the sea; even his smallfolk begged him to relent. Durran would have none of it. A seventh castle he raised, most massive of all. Some said the children of the forest helped him build it, shaping the stones with magic; others claimed that a small boy told him what he must do, a boy who would grow to be Bran the Builder. No matter how the tale was told, the end was the same. Though the angry gods threw storm after storm against it, the seventh castle stood defiant, and Durran Godsgrief and fair Elenei dwelt there together until the end of their days."

Storm's End • by Martina Pilcerova

Aegon's Garden • by Franz Miklis

Dragonstone Throne • by Marc Simonetti

"You wrong me, Onion Knight. Those were no fires of mine. Had I been with you, your battle would have had a different ending. But His Grace was surrounded by unbelievers, and his pride proved stronger than his faith. His punishment was grievous, but he has learned from his mistake."

–Melisandre, *A Storm of Swords*

Ser Davos Seaworth • by Mark Evans

"Davos had always been a sailor; he was meant to die at sea. *The gods beneath the waters have been waiting for me*, he told himself. *It's past time I went to them.*"

Ser Davos Seaworth • by Chris Dien

"Stannis had left his queen on Dragonstone along with her uncle Axell, but the queen's men were more numerous and powerful than ever, and Alester Florent was the foremost."

Alester Florent • by Roman V. Papsuev

Devan Seaworth • by Patrick McEvoy

"Devan was a good boy, but he wore the flaming heart proudly on his doublet, and his father had seen him at the nightfires as dusk fell, beseeching the Lord of Light to bring the dawn. He is the king's squire, he told himself, it is only to be expected that he would take the king's god."

Salladhor Saan • by Mark Evans

127

A Clash of Kings • by Stephen Youll

KING'S LANDING

It was on this shore that Aegon and his sisters first set foot on Westeros, and before long it grew into the greatest city in the Seven Kingdoms, many times larger than even the great cities of Lannisport and Oldtown. King's Landing contains multitudes: the high, the low, and everyone in between. The Gold Cloaks of the City Watch keep the peace as best they can.

In this city, the river Blackwater rushes; here is the Great Sept of Baelor, its seven crystal spires gleaming in the sun; here is Aegon's High Hill; here is the Red Keep, where the business of the realm is done; here are the slums of Flea Bottom; here is the plotting, treacherous heart of the Seven Kingdoms.

Here sits the Iron Throne, the sharp and dangerous seat of power forged from the swords of all the rulers who bent the knee to Aegon. Aegon had said that no man should rest easy on his throne.

The Iron Throne • by Tomasz Jedruszek

The Iron Throne • by Michael Komarck

"And above it all, frowning down from Aegon's high hill, was the Red Keep; seven huge drum-towers crowned with iron ramparts, an immense grim barbican, vaulted halls and covered bridges, barracks and dungeons and granaries, massive curtain walls studded with archers' nests, all fashioned of pale red stone. Aegon the Conqueror had commanded it built. His son Maegor the Cruel had seen it completed. Afterward he had taken the heads of every stonemason, woodworker, and builder who had labored on it. Only the blood of the dragon would ever know the secrets of the fortress the Dragonlords had built, he vowed."

The Red Keep • by Franz Miklis

Host of King's Landing • by Anders Finér

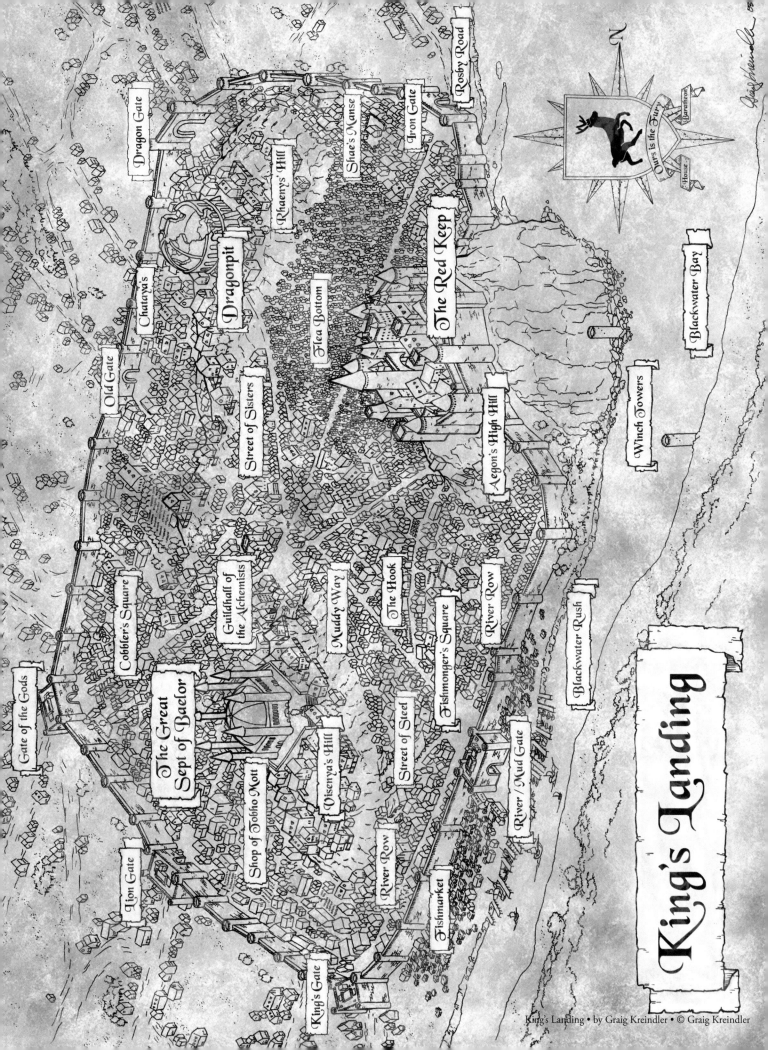

King's Landing • by Graig Kreindler • © Graig Kreindler

Ours is the Fury • House Baratheon

N

Dragon Gate

Rhaenys' Hill

Shae's Manse

Iron Gate

Rosby Road

Chataya's

Dragonpit

Flea Bottom

The Red Keep

Blackwater Bay

Old Gate

Street of Sisters

Aegon's High Hill

Winch Towers

Cobbler's Square

Guildhall of the Alchemists

Muddy Way

The Hook

Fishmonger's Square

River Row

Blackwater Rush

Gate of the Gods

The Great Sept of Baelor

Shop of Tobho Mott

Visenya's Hill

Street of Steel

River Row

Lion Gate

River / Mud Gate

Fishmarket

King's Gate

King's Landing

"He shouldered his way to where his daughter was seated and found her as the horns blew for the day's first joust. Sansa was so engrossed she scarcely seemed to notice his arrival."

Sansa's Favor • by Roman V. Papsuev

Cersei's Favor • by Roman V. Papsuev

"Last tourney, he dumped the Kingslayer on his golden rump, you ought to have seen the look on Cersei's face. I laughed till my sides hurt."

–Robert Baratheon, *A Game of Thrones*

"'Oberyn is toying with him,' said Ellaria Sand.

That is fool's play, thought Tyrion. 'The Mountain is too bloody big to be any man's toy.'"

Ellaria's Favor • by Roman V. Papsuev

"The maid was Loras Tyrell's sister Margaery, he'd confessed, but there were those who said she looked like Lyanna."

Margaery's Favor • by Roman V. Papsuev

"'My...queen,' Ser Jorah said, going to one knee. 'My sword that was his is yours, Daenerys. And my heart as well, that never belonged to your brother. I am only a knight, and I have nothing to offer you but exile, but I beg you, hear me.'"

Daenerys' Favor • by Roman V. Papsuev

Archery Contest • by Franz Vohwinkel

Asha's Contempt • by Roman V. Papsuev

"Asha was laughing at something one of her men had said, but broke off at his approach. 'Why, 'tis the Prince of Winterfell.' She tossed a bone to one of the dogs sniffing about the hall. Under that hawk's beak of a nose, her wide mouth twisted in a mocking grin. 'Or is it Prince of Fools?'"

Tourney for the Hand • by Michel Koch

"The jousting went all day and into the dusk, the hooves of the great warhorses pounding down the lists until the field was a ragged wasteland of torn earth. A dozen times Jeyne and Sansa cried out in unison as riders crashed together, lances exploding into splinters while the commons screamed for their favorites. Jeyne covered her eyes whenever a man fell, like a frightened little girl, but Sansa was made of sterner stuff. A great lady knew how to behave at tournaments."

House Swann Champion • by Mark Evans

"Cersei smiled the sort of smile she customarily reserved for Jaime. 'Lord Petyr, you are a wicked creature.'

'Thank you, Your Grace.'"

Littlefinger • by Michael Capprotti

Arrogant Lordling • by Jean Tay

Tourney Joust • by John Gravato

"'The sooner this folly is done with, the better I shall like it.' As if the expense and trouble were not irksome enough, all and sundry insisted on salting Ned's wound by calling it 'the Hand's tourney,' as if he were the cause of it. And Robert honestly seemed to think he should feel honored!"

Syrio Forel • by Don Maitz • © Don Maitz

"Littlefinger fingered his small pointed beard. 'You are slow to learn, Lord Eddard. Distrusting me was the wisest thing you've done since you climbed down off your horse.'"

Littlefinger • by Roman V. Papsuev • © Roman V. Papsuev

"'Treachery was a coin the Targaryens knew well,' Robert said. The anger was building in him again. 'Lannisters paid them back in kind. It was no less than they deserved. I shall not trouble my sleep over it.'"

Treachery • by John Matson

"The bells in the seven towers of the Great Sept of Baelor had tolled for a day and a night, the thunder of their grief rolling across the city in a bronze tide."

Great Sept of Baelor • by Bjarne Hansen

Take the White • by Marc Simonetti

Thoros of Myr • by Mark Evans

Varys • by Mark Evans

"Nothing happens in this city without Varys knowing. Oftimes he knows about it before it happens. He has informants everywhere. His little birds, he calls them."

–Littlefinger, *A Game of Thrones*

"'Do be careful, child,' Varys urged. 'King's Landing is not wholly safe these days. I know these streets well, and yet I almost feared to come today, alone and unarmed as I was. Lawless men are everywhere in this dark time, oh, yes. Men with cold steel and colder hearts.' Where I can come alone and unarmed, others can come with swords in their fists, he was saying."

Varys • by Michael Capprotti

"They left through a postern gate in the north wall. Tyrion put his heels into his horse and clattered down Shadowblack Lane. A few furtive shapes darted into alleys at the sound of hoofbeats on the cobbles, but no one dared accost them. The council had extended his curfew; it was death to be taken on the streets after the evenfall bells had sung."

Shadowblack Lane • by Franz Miklis

"Three hundred years ago, Catelyn knew, those heights had been covered with forest, and only a handful of fisherfolk had lived on the north sea. Then Aegon the Conqueror had sailed from Dragonstone. It was here that his army had put ashore, and there on the highest hill that he built his first crude redoubt of wood and earth."

Aegon's Hill • by Franz Miklis

Shae • by Jacques Bredy

"'The greater part of his foot remains at Bitterbridge.' Varys abandoned the brazier to take his seat at the table. 'Most of the lords who rode with Lord Renly to Storm's End have gone over banner-and-blade to Stannis, with all their chivalry.'"

Host of Renly's Shade • by Daarken

Stannis Baratheon • by Henning Ludvigsen

"The old maester looked at Stannis and saw only a man. You see a king. You are both wrong. He is the Lord's chosen, the warrior of fire. I have seen him leading the fight against the dark, I have seen it in the flames."

–Melisandre, *A Storm of Swords*

"With a knight of the Kingsguard as her sworn shield, no one is like to forget who or what she is."

–Tyrion Lannister, *A Clash of Kings*

Kingdom of Arms • by Jason Engle

Kingsguard • by Mark Evans

"They walked among the pavilions, each with its banner and its armor hung outside, the silence weighing heavier with every step."

Herald • by J. P. Targete

Counting Coppers • by Ted Pendergraft

"Spare me the foolishness, Maester. You know as well as I that the treasury has been empty for years. I shall have to borrow the money. No doubt the Lannisters will be accommodating. We owe Lord Tywin some three million dragons at present, what matter another hundred thousand?"

–Littlefinger, *A Game of Thrones*

"The High Septon once told me that as we sin, so do we suffer. If that's true, Lord Eddard, tell me...why is it always the innocents who suffer most, when you high lords play your game of thrones?"

–Varys, *A Game of Thrones*

High Septon • by Dean Broomfield

"The Street of Steel began at the market square beside the River Gate, as it was named on maps, or the Mud Gate, as it was commonly called."

River Gate • by Franz Miklis

"Every day since her escape from the Red Keep, Arya had visited each of the seven city gates in turn. The Dragon Gate, the Lion Gate, and the Old Gate were closed and barred. The Mud Gate and the Gate of the Gods were open, but only to those who wanted to enter the city; the guards let no one out."

Dragon Gate • by Franz Miklis

THE REACH

T he beauty of Highgarden is famous throughout the Seven Kingdoms: the pleasure boats that sail the River Mander, the fields of golden roses, and the countless gardens of autumn flowers. Luscious fruits are grown in the Reach: apples, grapes, fireplums, and peaches. The wines of the Arbor are prized everywhere there are civilized men.

This luxury is well-protected: the Tyrells of Highgarden command the largest army in the Seven Kingdoms, and they are well-versed in battle from their centuries-long grudge with the Dornishmen. Lord Tyrell and his mother Olenna–known at the Queen of Thorns–guard Highgarden's wealth, privilege, and pride with a ruthless intelligence.

Pleasure Barges of Highgarden • by Anders Finér

"'Your Grace,' Garlan said when the king approached him, 'I have a maiden sister, Margaery, the delight of our House. She was wed to Renly Baratheon, as you know, but Lord Renly went to war before the marriage could be consummated, so she remains innocent. Margaery has heard tales of your wisdom, courage, and chivalry, and has come to love you from afar. I beseech you to send for her, to take her hand in marriage, and to wed your House to mine for all time.'"

Margaery Tyrell • by Anders Finér

"'Bribes might sway some of the lesser lords,' Tyrion said, 'but never Highgarden.'"

Highgarden Envoy • by Sedone Thongvilay

"The wrinkled old lady smiled. 'At Highgarden we have many spiders amongst the flowers. So long as they keep to themselves we let them spin their little webs, but if they get underfoot we step on them.'"

Lady of Highgarden • by Sedone Thongvilay

Willas Tyrell • by Anders Finér

Knight of Flowers • by Jim Burns • © Jim Burns

Vanguard of the Rose • by Jason Engle

"Seventeen, and beautiful, and already a legend. Half the girls in the Seven Kingdoms wanted to bed him, and all the boys wanted to be him. 'If you will pardon my asking, ser - why would anyone choose to join the Kingsguard at seventeen?'"

Ser Loras Tyrell • by Jason Engle

"The Tyrells rose to power as the stewards to the Kings of the Reach, whose domain included the fertile plains of the southwest from the Dornish marches and the Blackwater Rush to the shores of the Sunset Sea."

Strength of Highgarden • by Tomasz Jedruszek

Knight of Flowers • by John Matson

"Ser Loras was the youngest son of Mace Tyrell, the Lord of Highgarden and Warden of the South. At sixteen, he was the youngest rider on the field, yet he had unhorsed three knights of the Kingsguard that morning in his first three jousts. Sansa had never seen anyone so beautiful. His plate was intricately fashioned and enameled as a bouquet of a thousand different flowers, and his snow-white stallion was draped in a blanket of red and white roses."

Rainbow Guard • by Jason Engle

Rose Gardens • by Anders Finér

DORNE

Descended from the Rhoynar, and the last to bend the knee to the Targaryen throne, the Dornish are a fiercely independent people. Their lands are varied, encompassing mountains, deserts, and coast. Pomegranates grow here, as do olives, lemons, and plums.

House Martell traces its lineage back to the legendary warrior queen Nymeria. This proud heritage was never forgotten, and the Dornish were never conquered by Aegon, only joining the Seven Kingdoms two hundred years after the Conquest, marrying into the ruling family.

Later still, Princess Elia Martell was wed to Rhaegar Targaryen–but she was murdered, along with her children, by The Mountain That Rides, Ser Gregor Clegane, in the last days of Robert's Rebellion. The Dornish lust for vengeance is legendary, and it is doubtful that this atrocity will be forgotten.

The Fountains of Dorne • by Anders Finér

"Ser Gregor's huge hands, clad in gauntlets of lobstered steel, clasped the crosshilt to either side of the grip. Even Prince Oberyn's paramour paled at the sight of him. 'You are going to fight that?' Ellaria Sand said in a hushed voice.

'I am going to kill that,' her lover replied carelessly."

Prince Oberyn Martell • by Roman V. Papsuev • © Roman V. Papsuev

"He was sending Ser Arys Oakheart as her sworn shield, and had engaged the Braavosi to bring her the rest of the way to Sunspear. Even Lord Stannis would hesitate to wake the anger of the greatest and most powerful of the Free Cities."

Sunspear • by Roberto Marchesi

"Ellaria's girls are too young to be a danger, but there are those who might seek to use them against me."

–Doran Martell, *A Feast for Crows*

Ellaria Sand • by Xia Taptara

Two Steps Ahead • by Jean Tay

Nymeria Sand • by Dennis Calero

"Nymeria Sand was five-and-twenty, and slender as a willow. Her straight black hair, worn in a long braid bound up with red-gold wire, made a widow's peak above her dark eyes, just as her father's had. With her high cheekbones, full lips, and milk-pale skin, she had all the beauty that her elder sister lacked...but Obara's mother had been an Oldtown whore, whilst Nym was born from the noblest blood of old Volantis."

"Lady Tyene's voice was gentle, and she looked as sweet as summer strawberries. Her mother had been a septa, and Tyene had an air of almost otherworldly innocence about her."

Tyene Sand • by Xia Taptara

"Lady Nym was no less deadly, though she kept her knives well-hidden."

Nymeria Sand • by John Gravato

"As they were crossing the yard, Prince Oberyn of Dorne fell in beside them, his black-haired paramour on his arm. Sansa glanced at the woman curiously. She was baseborn and unwed, and had two bastard daughters for the prince, but she did not fear to look even the queen in the eye. Shae had told her that this Ellaria worshiped some Lysene love goddess. 'She was almost a whore when he found her, m'lady,' her maid confided, 'and now she's near a princess.'"

Paramour • by Sedone Thongvilay

"Princess Arianne strode to the litter on snakeskin sandals laced up to her thighs. Her hair was a mane of jet-black ringlets that fell to the small of her back, and around her brow was a band of copper suns. *She is still a little thing,* the captain thought. Where the Sand Snakes were tall, Arianne took after her mother, who stood but five foot two. Yet beneath her jeweled girdle and loose layers of flowing purple silk and yellow samite she had a woman's body, lush and roundly curved."

Obara Sand • by Martina Pilcerova

"Obara was the eldest Sand Snake, a big-boned woman near to thirty, with the close-set eyes and rat-brown hair of the Oldtown whore who'd birthed her. Beaneath a mottled sandsilk cloak of dun and gold, her riding clothes were old brown leather, worn and supple. They were the softest things about her."

Dornish Riders • by John Gravato

"Dorne was the last of the Seven Kingdoms to swear fealty to the Iron Throne. Blood, custom, and history all set the Dornishmen apart from the other kingdoms."

Horsemen of Starfall • by Tomasz Jedruszek

Dornish Lancer • by Uwe Jarling

"Obara is too loud...Obara would make Oldtown our father's funeral pyre, but I am not so greedy..."

–Nymeria Sand, *A Feast for Crows*

Obara Sand • by Eric Wilkerson

"A bolder man might roll the dice for Dorne. If he should win Sunspear to his cause, he might prolong this war for years. So we will not offend the Martells any further, for any reason."

–Tywin Lannister, *A Storm of Swords*

Halls of Sunspear • by Roberto Marchesi

"'The sands were duly grateful.' Dayne put a foot upon the head of a statue that might have been the Maiden till the sands had scoured her away."

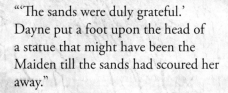

Desert Cache • by Eric Wilkerson

Rhoynar Monument • by Shane Watson

Sunspear • by Martina Pilcerova

THE FREE CITIES & THE EAST

To the east of Westeros lies another, larger continent, where many marvelous and strange things are to be found.

The Nine Free Cities are well-known to the men of the west, and the nomadic hordes of the Dothraki are not completely alien to them. The west knows of the poisoners of Lys, and the Faceless Men of Braavos, and a man of Myr was even a favorite friend of King Robert. But beyond these, further east, lie Yi Ti, Qarth, Asshai by the Shadow, and the Jade Sea. Here knowledge fades, and understanding dims.

It is to these lands that the last of the Targaryens, Daenerys and Viserys, fled after the rebellion. It is here that a new Targaryen army is rising, poised to reclaim Westeros from the usurpers, wielding the mighty weapon of Aegon the Conqueror: dragons.

Titan of Braavos • by Jim Burns • © Jim Burns

"Ten thousand, that would be enough, I could sweep the Seven Kingdoms with ten thousand Dothraki screamers. The realm will rise for its rightful king."

–Viserys Targaryen, *A Game of Thrones*

Thundering Cavalry • by Torstein Nordstrand

Bloodthirsty Khal • by Mike Franchina

"Drogo's braid was black as midnight and heavy with scented oil, hung with tiny bells that rang softly as he moved. It swung well past his belt, below even his buttocks, the end of it brushing against the back of his thighs."

Khal Drogo • by John Matson

"'You see how long it is?' Viserys said. 'When Dothraki are defeated in combat, they cut off their braids in disgrace, so the world will know their shame. Khal Drogo has never lost a fight. He is Aegon the Dragonlord come again, and you will be his queen.'"

Khal Drogo • by Mark Evans

Khal Drogo • by John Matson

"She was Daenerys Stormborn, the Unburnt, *khaleesi* and queen, Mother of Dragons, slayer of warlocks, breaker of chains, and there was no one in the world that she could trust."

Daenerys Targaryen • by John Matson

Queen Dany's Command • by Tomasz Jedruszek

"Rakharo...you shall have the great arakh that was my bride gift, with hilt and blade chased in gold. And you too I name my ko, and ask that you live and die as blood of my blood, riding at my side to keep me safe from harm."

–Daenerys Targaryen, *A Game of Thrones*

Rakharo • by Roman V. Papsuev

Mother of Dragons • by Socar Myles

Fire and Blood • by Thomas Gianni

Hatchlings • by Patrick McEvoy

Blood of the Dragon • by Franz Vohwinkel

"As swift as the wind he rides, and behind him his khalasar covers the earth, men without number, with arakhs shining in their hands like blades of razor grass. Fierce as a storm this prince will be. His enemies will tremble before him, and their wives will weep tears of blood and rend their flesh in grief. The bells in his hair will sing his coming, and the milk men in the stone tents will fear his name."

–Crone of Vaes Dothrak, *A Game of Thrones*

Drogo's Khalasar • by Tomasz Jedruszek

"Beyond the horse gate, plundered gods and stolen heroes loomed to either side of them. The forgotten deities of dead cities brandished their broken thunderbolts at the sky as Dany roder her silver past their feet. Stone kings looked down on her from their thrones, their faces chipped and stained, even their names lost in the mists of time."

Graveyard of the Gods • by Patrick Keith

Bloodriders • by Tomasz Jedruszek

Valar Morghulis • by Thomas Denmark

"Cursing her softly, the man went to a knee to grope for the coin in the dirt and there was his neck right in front of her. Arya slid her dagger out and drew it across his throat, as smooth as summer silk. His blood covered her hands in a hot gush and he tried to shout but there was blood in his mouth as well.

'Valar morghulis,' she whispered as he died."

The Unsullied • by Franz Vohwinkel

Meereen • by Martina Pilcerova

Lys • by Martina Pilcerova

"We can make a slave of you as well, do not doubt it. There are pleasure houses in Lys and Tyrosh where men would pay handsomely to bed the last Targaryen."

–Grazdan Mo Erat, *A Storm of Swords*

Qartheen Bazaar • by Martina Pilcerova

Ser Jorah Mormont • by Jacques Bredy

The Dothraki Sea • by Eric Wilkerson

"'If walls could keep us small, peasants would all be tiny and kings as large as giants,' said Ser Jorah. 'I've seen huge men born in hovels, and dwarfs who dwelt in castles.'

'Men are men,' Whitebeard replied. 'Dragons are dragons.'

Ser Jorah snorted his disdain. 'How profound.' The exiled knight had no love for the old man, he'd made that plain from the first. 'What do you know of dragons, anyway?'"

Astapor • by Martina Pilcerova

181

"And there was Quaithe of the Shadow, that strange woman in the red lacquer mask with all her cryptic counsel. Was she an enemy too, or only a dangerous friend? Dany could not say."

Army of Light • by Scott Keating

Quaithe of the Shadows • by Xia Taptara

"'I am Belwas. Strong Belwas they named me in the fighting pits of Meereen. Never did I lose.' He slapped his belly, covered with scars. 'I let each man cut me once, before I kill him. Count the cuts and you will know how many Strong Belwas has slain.'"

Strong Belwas • by Mark Evans

Daenerys Targaryen • by Esad Ribic • © Esad Ribic

ARTIST BIOS

Allan Bednar

Allan Bednar was born in Chicago, but moved to the UK at the age of 15, where he happily resides with his wife Charis and their two children. He has worked for a number of game companies and publishers. More of his work can be seen at http://allanbednargallery.mysite. wanadoo-members.co.uk/. Alongside freelance illustration, he is currently working on a degree in psychology.

Dean Bloomfield

Dean Bloomfield has created artwork for Fantasy Flight Games and Torchlight Games, among other clients. His work can be viewed online at www.loadedpixels.com.

Jim Burns

Jim Burns' works are striking for their 'larger-than-life' portrayals of scenes of the far future, and in particular for his fantastic 'hardware'. His masterful technique depicts land, sky, and space vehicles in gleaming metal and plastic so perfectly painted that one senses one can actually feel the metallic touch of chrome or smell the pungent odour of plastic in his work.

He is constantly in demand for UK book covers, although more recently his work is being commissioned by American publishing houses. Apart from book and game covers, Burns worked with Ridley Scott on *Blade Runner*. He has also had books of his own works published: *Lightship*, *Planet Story* (written by Harry Harrison), *Mechanismo*, *Transluminal*, and many others.

Thomas Denmark

Thomas has worked as a concept artist and a modeler/ texture artist on games published by Electronic Arts, LucasArts, and Accolade. He is currently a freelance illustrator with a diverse list of clients including White Wolf Studio, Humanhead Studios, Alderac Entertainment Group, Decipher, Paizo Publishing, and others. His work can be viewed online at www.studiodenmark. com.

Chris Dien

Chris Dien has always loved drawing since early childhood, but never considered a career in art. After graduating from high school, Chris served three years in the U.S. Army. Then he completed his bachelor's degree in business. During this time, Chris taught himself how to paint and draw. Upon seeing some of his work on the internet, Chris was approached by a card game company to produce art for their collectible card game. Since then he has gone on to work professionally doing illustrations for card games and roleplaying games for various publishers in the industry.

Jenny Dolfen

Jenny Dolfen was born in Bremerhaven in northern Germany. After finishing school (and drawing all the while) she went on to become a teacher of English and Latin, but has started illustrating full-time since the birth of her son (or as full-time as a baby will allow). She now lives near Aachen in the west of Germany with her husband, who is an avid gamer, and their son, who is showing first signs of being very fond of dragons.

Jason Engle

Jason has been making art professionally, in one medium or another, for about seven years. However, he has been making art as a hobby for most of his life. He knew at a very young age that he wanted to be an artist, and pursued that goal with every free moment.

Born in southern California in 1979, he was raised by very encouraging and supportive parents on a ranch in Arizona until the age of 18. He never attended a major university or art academy of any kind, and he's always found the best teacher in art to be experience itself. With that in mind, he found a job in commercial art and design, and moved to Florida to begin his career. This is not an indication that Florida is a good place to start an art career, quite the opposite, but it did have one major thing in its favor. There was a company there willing to hire him. Also, it has lots of beaches.

Mark Evans

Since graduating from Pratt Institute in 1991 on a Full Scholarship, Mark Evans has spent his days, nights, and weekends inside his "lab" producing storyboards, concept designs, and production illustration for commercials and film. He has been lucky enough to work on major campaigns with advertising agencies and clients from Seattle to Germany, and hopes to expand his work in the sci-fi, fantasy, and horror genres in the coming years.

He lives in NYC with his lucky black cat Dave, his Macintosh computer, and a massive collection of comics.

Anders Finér

Anders Finér is a self-taught artist born in Torsby, Sweden. He has worked with art for comic books, CCG and RPG games, graphic novels, computer games, and CG commercials. Some of his titles include: *The Seventh Shrine*, *The Hedge Knight*, *Arkham Horror*, *The Longest Journey*, and *Free Jimmy*. At the present time he is working at an animation studio, as a CG painter in Oslo, Norway.

Donato Giancola

Donato Giancola was born in 1967 and raised in Colchester, Vermont. He attended Syracuse University where he graduated Summa Cum Laude in 1992. Donato has taught, lectured, and sold hundreds of paintings worldwide. He is best known for his realistic, stunning portrayals of J.R.R. Tolkien's *Lord of the Rings* characters.

Donato's work can be viewed online at www.donatoart.com. He currently lives in Brooklyn.

Thomas Gianni

Born, raised, and educated in Chicago, Thomas majored in illustration and figure drawing at the American Academy of Art. His early influences were comic book and fantasy artists such as Jack Kirby (*Fantastic Four and Hulk*), Will Eisner (*The Spirit*), Steve Ditko (*Spider Man*), Jim Steranko (*Nick Fury*), and of course, Frank Frazetta.

John Howe

John Howe was born in 1957 in Vancouver, Canada, and after leaving high school, he went to an American college in France to learn French. He then enrolled at the Ecoles des Arts Décoratifs de Strasbourg, where he remained for three years, before moving to Switzerland to work on animated film. He is famous for his work on J.R.R. Tolkien's *Lord of the Rings*, and was a concept artist for the Peter Jackson movie trilogy. He now lives and works in Switzerland as a freelance illustrator, with wife Fataneh and son Dana. His work can be viewed online at www.john-howe.com.

Uwe Jarling

Every serious artist's biography really should start with the sentence: "I'm drawing since I'm able to hold a pencil!!!" because it's nothing but the real truth. And it sure was the same in Uwe's case. He just never laid the pencil down after having grabbed it once.

Uwe has made covers for movies based on novels by Steven King, George Romero, Alexandre Dumas, Charles Dickens, Rudyard Kipling, Arthur Conan Doyle, Frances Burnett, and many more. He also has made cover illustrations for several books by publishers, like Bastei Lübbe and Fischer, to mention the most popular, as well as many technical and architectural illustrations for advertising agencies. His work can be viewed online at www.jarling-arts.com.

Michael Komarck

Michael Komarck was born in Louisiana and promptly relocated to Michigan where he's lived ever since. As the years passed, he transitioned from crayons to pencils to acrylics to oils, and in 1989 he found himself at a community college where his suspicions that he was better off self-taught in art were proven correct almost immediately. His stint there was brief in the extreme.

After several years as a projectionist at the local Cineplex, he co-founded a small publishing company. However, with the exception of illustrating several children's books, the majority of his time was spent designing business cards, ads, and eventually web-related materials (mostly Flash animation). It was during this period that he was introduced to Photoshop and ultimately replaced his oils with digital paint. Eventually he left to pursue a career as a full-time illustrator. He spent a couple years building a portfolio while designing business/self-help book covers to pay the bills (to this day he still happily designs several such covers a year).

The door was opened for Michael in 2003 when Meisha Merlin Publishing offered him cover work for authors, including Robert Asprin and George R.R. Martin. Michael's work can be seen online at www.komarckart.com.

Graig Kreindler

Graig Kreindler, born in 1980, grew up in Rockland County, New York. He recently graduated from the School of Visual Arts in New York City with a BFA in Illustration. His award-winning sports work has appeared in juried shows in New York City, Philadelphia, and Los Angeles, as well as having been featured in a nationally distributed magazine.

His paintings depict a variety of subjects, including fantasy, portraiture, and landscapes, though his passion is sports illustration, with a particular focus on historical baseball subject matter. To Graig, no other sport embodies the relationship between generations and the sense of community like baseball. His goal is to portray the national pastime in an era in which players were accessibly human, and the atmosphere of a cozy ballpark was just as important as what happened on the field.

Don Maitz

Enthusiastic reception and international acclaim have surrounded the imaginative paintings of Don Maitz for nearly 30 years. Don Maitz has received two Hugo awards, a special Hugo for Best Original Artwork, a Howard Award, the Silver Medal of Excellence from the Society of Illustrators, the Inkpot Award, and ten Chesley Awards for his creative efforts.

His images adorn books, magazines, cards, limited edition prints, puzzles, computer screen savers, and other merchandise. Two art books of his work have been produced, *Dreamquests: The Art of Don Maitz* and *First Maitz*. He is featured in the first *Fantasy Art Masters* book and is its cover artist. His work can be found in all Spectrum books, save one. His paintings have been exhibited at NASA's 25th Anniversary Show, the Park Avenue Atrium, the Hayden Planetarium, Society of Illustrators, the New Britain Museum of American Art,

Delaware Art Museum, the Canton Art Museum, the Key West Museum of Art & History, the San Diego Maritime Museum, and the Florida International Museum.

Maitz created and continues the Captain Morgan Spiced Rum character, and has worked as a conceptual artist on the animated feature films *Jimmy Neutron: Boy Genius* and *Ant Bully*. His web site is www.paravia.com/DonMaitz.

John Matson

John Matson developed his love of fantasy and science fiction at an early age, regularly covering his school folders and homework with doodles of an alien and barbarian persuasion. Born and raised in Milwaukee, Wisconsin, he attended Milwaukee High School of the Arts and graduated in 1994 from the Milwaukee Institute of Art and Design (MIAD) with a BFA in illustration. After living in Texas for a few years, John moved back to Milwaukee in 1999, where in addition to a sometimes hectic freelance schedule he now teaches what was his favorite class at MIAD.

Franz Miklis

Born on June 12th, 1963, in Oberndorf bei Salzburg, Austria, Franz Miklis studied at the International Summer Academy and has been a science fiction and fantasy artist since 1980. His published work includes *Alien Contact*, *Andromeda*, *A Game of Thrones*, *Between the Stars*, and hundreds of others, in addition to dozens of international exhibitions.

His favorite commission so far was his work for the *A Game of Thrones* collectible card game, for which he painted 60 unique locations of the fabulous world of Westeros. He is a member of "The New Masters of Fantasy," and is living near Salzburg with his wife Monika and his two children.

Mike S. Miller

Mike S. Miller was born in Hawaii and grew up in San Jose, California. He's been in the comics industry for over 10 years and has worked for various companies such as Marvel on *X-Men* and DC Comics on *Adventures of Superman*, and also for Image and Malibu. Mike is best known among *A Song of Ice and Fire* fans for his stunning illustration for the comic adaptation of the Hedge Knight short story.

Socar Myles

Socar Myles likes rats, drawings, and, not surprisingly, drawings with rats in them. She also likes springtime, the outdoors, and the way grape juice tastes when one is incredibly thirsty. Her favorite hobby is playing huge, elaborate practical jokes. There's not much else to say about Socar Myles, except that she's an illustrator living in BC, Canada.

Torstein Nordstrand

Living in Norway, Torstein is one of many illustrators taking advantage of the new digital age to freelance for gaming companies all over the world. Having started his career as a painter sometime in the last millennium, his paintings can now be found in the publications of many major publishers of fantasy entertainment, usually in the form of card art and interior illustration. In the unlikey hour when he is not painting fervently, he highly enjoys travelling the world, appreciating the creative efforts of others, and spending time with his forgiving wife Christine. To see more of Torstein's work, visit www.torsteinnordstrand.com.

Roman V. Papsuev

Roman Papsuev worked in a travel agency and went all the way up from simple agent to financial director, but his love of art made him quit his main job for the adventure of freelancing. Since 2003 he's worked non-stop on illustrating books, RPG games, CCG games, and some other work just for the fun of it. He's a self-taught artist and never received any professional education. He loves his job and considers himself a very lucky man. He lives in Moscow, and loves to read and watch movies.

Martina Pilcerova

Martina Pilcerova was born in Czechoslovakia and she has been painting for publishers since 1988. She received her Master Degree in Fine Arts in Bratislava in 2001. Her works have appeared on more than 80 covers of books and magazines all around the world. She won the Jack Gaughan Award and multiple Best Science Fiction and Fantasy Artist in Czech Republic and Slovakia.

Her latest paintings are done mostly for the gaming industry: *A Game of Thrones* collectible card game, *Magic the Gathering,* and *Dungeons & Dragons.* She worked on two movie productions, including cooperation with Volker Engel, creator of special effects on *Independence Day.* She also works on her own illustrated novel.

Esad Ribic

Esad Ribic is a professional illustrator, perhaps best known for his work in comics. His work has also appeared on the covers of the Croatian edition of *A Clash of Kings* and *A Storm of Swords.*

John Schoenherr

After graduating in 1956, John Schoenherr established a career as an illustrator. Throughout the 1960s and much of the 1970s, he illustrated over forty books, including Sterling North's *Rascal* (1963), Jean Craighead George's *Julie of the Wolves* (1971) and Frank Herbert's *Dune* (1977), in addition to producing covers for *Reader's Digest* and *Astounding Science Fiction.*

A member of the American Society of Mammalogists and the Society of Animal Artists, Schoenherr has exhibited his paintings throughout the United States. He has continued his activity as an illustrator, as well, winning the prestigious Caldecott Medal in 1988 for his work in *Owl Moon.* He has also written and illustrated two children's books. A major retrospective of his work, *John Schoenherr: Beyond the Edge and Deep Within,* was held at the Hiram Blauvelt Art Museum in Oradell, New Jersey, in 1997.

Marc Simonetti

Marc Simonetti was born in 1977 in Lyon, France. After a very short engineering career, he studied art at the Emile Cohl School of Arts. He now works as a freelancer, dividing his time between creating illustrations for books, RPGs, and collectible card games, and making 3D backgrounds (modeling and texturing) and concept art for video games.

Jamie Sims

Jamie Sims is a professional illustrator who drew the concept sketches for the Testor Corporation miniatures based on the *A Song of Ice and Fire* novels.

Steve Stone

Steve Stone was born in Manchester in 1964 and abandoned his football skills for art at the age of 17. By 1985, he had graduated with a 2-1 BA Honours in Fine Art from Trent Polytechnic School of Art.

Steve's ambitious character led him straight into film-making, and his debut animation *Where is She Babe* landed him the opportunity to take his work to America after it was spotted by events company Tense Productions. Ten years later, after working extensively in the US with cutting edge computer technology running light shows and montage video projections, Steve returned to the UK and set up graphics company Nexus DNA.

Now living in South Yorkshire with wife Sian and daughter Claudia, Steve is one of the most respected fantasy artists of his generation, constantly working in publishing and other markets and receiving commissions from around the world.

Represented by Artist Partners Ltd. www.artistpartners. com - Steve Stone - www.nexus-dna.demon.co.uk.

Xia Taptara

Xia Taptara (AKA Hwang XiaoZhen) currently lives in beautiful, cloudy Seattle, WA...the forever rainy and foggy city. He can't really remember when he picked up the first crayon and began to draw or scribble. When he was little his ultimate dream was to be a comic book artist and/or make art in video games. In 1999 he decided to pursue the childish dream and seriously work on becoming a good commercial artist. In 2001 he got his foot in the door as a 2D character animator with a local company making Disney titles video games. In late 2002 he learned how to paint digitally with Photoshop and 3D modelling in Max and Maya. Currently, Xia works full-time at ArenaNet as a 3D character modeler. He love his job, beautiful ladies, cute waitresses, all his ex-girlfriends, bad movies, retro video games, doodling, and of course a good icy cold beer.

J. P. Targete

Sought after by publishers for its meticulous rendering and dynamic colors, Targete's art can be found on book covers for Avon books, Berkley/Ace Ballantine, Bantam, Tor, and a host of others. His art has been displayed in the Spectrum annuals "The Best in Contemporary Fantastic Art." In 1999, his painting *Wrapt in Crystal*, for the book by Sharon Shinn, was nominated for a Chesley Award, and in 2000 his book cover painting *Circle at Center*, for the book by Douglas Niles, won a Chesley Award for best paperback cover.

Presently Jean Pierre Targete works and lives as a freelance illustrator in Miami, Florida. His work can be found on your local bookstore shelves in his first art book *Illumina: The Art of J.P. Targete*, published by Paper Tiger.

Charles Vess

Charles was born in 1951 in Lynchburg, Virginia, and has been drawing since he could hold a crayon. He drew his first full-length comic when he was 10 and called it *Atomic Man*. Minimalist in nature, it required no drawing of hands, feet, or heads ("they just glowed"). Since then, he has painstakingly drawn thousands of hands, feet, and heads in great detail. Charles graduated with a BFA from Virginia Commonwealth University, and worked in commercial animation for Candy Apple Productions in Richmond, Virginia, before moving to New York City in 1976.

His award-winning work has graced the pages of numerous comic book publishers, such as Marvel, DC, Dark Horse, and Epic. He has been featured in several gallery and museum exhibitions across the nation, including the first major exhibition of Science Fiction and Fantasy Art (New Britain Museum of American Art, 1980) and "Dreamweavers" (William King Regional Arts Center, 1994-95).

In 1991, Charles shared the prestigious World Fantasy Award for Best Short Story with Neil Gaiman for their collaboration on *Sandman #19* (DC Comics) – the first and only time a comic book has held this honor. In the summer of 1997, Charles won the Will Eisner Comic Industry Award for Best Penciler/Inker for his work on *The Book of Ballads and Sagas* (which he self-published through his own Green Man Press), as well as *Sandman*

#75. In 2002 Charles won a second Will Eisner Award, this time as Best Painter for his work on *Rose*, a 130-page epic fantasy saga written by Cartoon Books' Jeff Smith.

Charles is currently hard at work producing drawings for several new books, including, *A Storm of Swords* (Meisha Merlin), the 25th anniversary edition of *Moonheart* (Subterranean Press), and a graphic novel collection of his ballad material for Tor.

Franz Vohwinkel

Franz Vohwinkel was born in 1964 in Munich, Germany. He studied graphic design in Darmstadt and received his diploma in 1991. In the same year, he also illustrated his very first game: *Drunter & Drüber* by Klaus Teuber. Since then, he has done illustration and graphic design for over 200 games.

Among his personal highlights are the illustrations for the latest edition of the *Classic Battletech* Box Set, the first German TCG *Behind*, and his work for *Dungeons & Dragons* and *Blue Moon*. In recent years he has illustrated cards for the trading card games *Warlord, Legends of the Five Rings, WarCry, Warhammer 40K, Horus Heresy, A Game of Thrones*, and a few book covers. Three of his illustrations for *Classic Battletech* were shown in *Spectrum: The Best in Contemporary Fantastic Art*.

Franz Vohwinkel lives and works with his wife in Ottobrunn, near Munich.

Shane Watson

S.C.Watson is a freelance artist living in the Pacific Northwest. His interests are too many to mention, but his primary love (aside from his wife and kids) is painting. More of his works can be found at www.oregano-productions.com.

Stephen Youll

Stephen Youll was born in Hartlepool, England, in 1965. At a very early age he knew he wanted to become an artist. Stephen graduated from Durham New College of Art and Design, and then furthered his art education at Sunderland University. To help pay for much-needed art materials, Steve would enter and win art contests. He also was taking on professional advertising work in the evenings and on weekends while working on his degree.

Stephen Youll's art can be found on many hardback and paperback book covers. The many companies he has worked for include Bantam Books, Warner Books, Tor Books, Avon Books, Ballentine Books, Penguin Books, Daw Books, DC Comics, and the IBM Corporation. He has illustrated covers for many famous authors, including Arthur C. Clark, C.J. Cherryh, Robert Silverberg, Margaret Weis and Tracy Hickman, Ben Bova, Kevin J. Anderson, Ian McDonald, Harry Turtledove, Michael Stackpole, David Feintuch, George R. R. Martin, Robin Hobb, Brian Herbert, and many others, notably Isaac Asimov. He has also illustrated six *Star Wars* books; the first one, *Tales from the Mos Eisley Cantina*, became the bestselling science fiction anthology of all time.

Stephen Youll has also shown and exhibited his work throughout the United States and England and been awarded with many ribbons at conventions, which include Best Artist, Best in Show, and Best Professional Artist. Stephen Youll currently lives in New Jersey with his wife and cat.

Ryan Barger, Linda Bergkvist, Jacques Bredy, Manuel Calderon, Dennis Calero, Michael Capprotti, Jhoneil Centeno, Miguel Coimbra, Daarken, Allen Douglas, Emrah Elmasli, Mike Franchina, John Gravato, Cris Griffin, Daerick Gross Sr., Nils Hamm, Bjarne Hansen, Christian Iken, Tomasz Jedruszek, Scott Keating, Patrick Keith, Michel Koch, Henning Ludvigsen, Roberto Marchesi, Patrick McEvoy, Andrew Navaro, Jim Pavelic, Ted Pendergraft, Natascha Roeoesli, Jean Tay, Sedone Thongvilay, Tim Truman, and Eric Wilkerson are all professional artists who have contributed to the *A Game of Thrones* collectible card game.